Winter Punches to Nut Crunches

by **Marilyn LaPenta**

Consultant:
Mandi Pek, MS, RD, CSP, CDN

PUBLISHING

NEW YORK, NEW YORK

Credits

All food illustrations by Kim Jones

Publisher: Kenn Goin
Editor: Joy Bean
Creative Director: Spencer Brinker
Design: Debrah Kaiser

Library of Congress Cataloging-in-Publication Data

La Penta, Marilyn.
    Winter punches to nut crunches / by Marilyn LaPenta.
        pages cm. — (Yummy tummy recipes: seasons)
Audience: Ages 7-12.
Includes bibliographical references and index.
ISBN 978-1-61772-743-6 (library binding) — ISBN 1-61772-743-1 (library binding)
1. Seasonal cooking—Juvenile literature. 2. Winter—Juvenile literature. I. Title.
TX652.5.L284 2013
641.5'64—dc23

2012037780

For more information, write to Bearport Publishing Company, Inc., 45 West 21st Street, Suite 3B, New York, New York, 10010. Printed in the United States of America.

10 9 8 7 6 5 4 3 2 1

Contents

Making Healthy Winter Snacks 4

Getting Started 6

Warm Cranberry Punch 8

Perfect Pumpkin Nog 9

Peppermint Hot Chocolate 10

Here We Come A-Wassailing Punch 11

Valentine Pink Hot Cocoa 12

St. Patrick's Day Green Smoothie 13

Sleepy Time Milk Tea 14

Apple Nut Oatmeal 15

Quick Corn Chowder 16

Butternut Squash Soup 17

Ginger Cookies 18

Yummy Coconut Balls 19

Nut-and-Honey Bars 20

Nutty Crunchy Granola 21

Healthy Tips 22

Glossary 23

Index 24

Bibliography 24

Read More 24

Learn More Online 24

About the Author 24

Making Healthy Winter Snacks

Get ready to make some yummy winter snacks. All the recipes in *Winter Punches to Nut Crunches* make delicious cold-weather treats.

You can eat well throughout the winter by enjoying fresh fruits and vegetables such as cranberries, pumpkins, and squashes. You can find these foods at farmers' markets or nearby farms. If fresh food isn't available, frozen fruits and vegetables are a good substitute.

The great thing about making your own winter drinks, snacks, and soups is that you can choose exactly what goes into each recipe. You'll also avoid many of the **preservatives** found in **pre-made** foods that are not always good for your body. Use the ideas on page 22 to make the nutritious dishes in this book even healthier. There you will find ways to reduce fat and sugar in recipes, which can lead to **obesity**.

Getting Started

Use these cooking tips and safety and tool guidelines to make the best punches and nut crunches you've ever tasted.

Tips

Here are a few tips to get your cooking off to a great start.

- Quickly check out the Prep Time, Cooking Time, Tools, and Servings information at the top of each recipe. It will tell you how long the recipe takes to prepare, the tools you'll need, and the number of people the recipe serves.

- Once you pick a recipe, set out the tools and ingredients that you will need on your worktable.

- Before and after cooking, wash your hands well with warm soapy water to kill any germs.

- Wash fruits and vegetables as appropriate to get rid of any dirt and chemicals.

- Put on an apron or smock to protect your clothes.

- Roll up long shirtsleeves to keep them clean.

- Tie back long hair or cover it to keep it out of the food.

- *Very Important:* Keep the adults happy and clean up the kitchen when you've finished cooking.

PREP TIME COOKING TIME TOOLS SERVINGS

INGREDIENTS

RECIPE

15 Minutes Prep Time **20–25** Minutes Cooking Time Tools **21** Bars

Ingredients

Cooking spray
½ cup cashews
1 ½ cups pumpkin seeds

1 cup almonds
½ cup sunflower seeds
1 cup dried cranraisins

1 teaspoon cinnamon
½ cup honey
¼ cup butter (½ stick)

Steps

1. **Preheat** the oven to 350°F. Coat a 9 X 13-inch casserole dish with cooking spray.
2. Have an adult set up the food processor with the S blade. Put the cashews, 1 cup of the pumpkin seeds, and the almonds into the food processor. **Grind** into flour (about 40 seconds). Don't grind too long or the mixture will turn into butter.
3. With the mixing spoon, put the nut flour into a medium bowl. Add the sunflower seeds, ½ cup of pumpkin seeds, cranraisins, and cinnamon into the bowl and stir.
4. On the stovetop, put the butter and honey in a pot and heat until the butter melts.
5. Carefully remove the pot from the stovetop with the potholders and pour the honey mixture over the nut mixture. Stir until everything is evenly coated.
6. Pour the mixture into the casserole dish. Use a wet spoon to spread it evenly.
7. Bake for 20 to 25 minutes, until it is lightly browned on top.
8. Carefully remove the dish from the oven with the pot holders. Let the mixture cool for 20 minutes, then gently cut it into bars. Allow the bars to cool completely before removing them from the pan with a spatula.

Cashews are in the same family as poison ivy and poison sumac. They have chemical irritants, but those are only found in the shell and not in the nut itself. To make sure that the cashews are free of these irritants, manufacture roast the nuts at a very high temperature.

Be Safe

Cook safely by having an adult around to help with these activities:

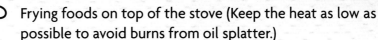 Using a sharp knife or peeler

Using the stove, microwave, blender, or other electrical appliances

Removing hot pans from the oven (*Always* use pot holders.)

Frying foods on top of the stove (Keep the heat as low as possible to avoid burns from oil splatter.)

Tools You Need

Here's a guide to the tools you will need to make the various recipes in this book.

Spoon

Mixing spoon

Slotted spoon

Knife

Measuring cups

Measuring spoons

Peeler

Whisk

Cutting board

Rolling pin

Spatula

Ladle

Mugs

Small dish

Medium glass, 12 ounces

Soup bowl

Small bowl

Medium Bowl

Large bowl

Punch bowl

Pot holders

Plastic bag

Wax paper

Grater

Colander

Pot

Cookie sheet

9" x 13" casserole dish

Wire rack

Refrigerator

Stovetop

Oven

Microwave

Food processor

Blender

Electric mixer

Warm Cranberry Punch

Tools

35 Minutes Prep Time

20 Servings

Ingredients

8 cups water

¾ cup honey

3 whole cloves

3 cinnamon sticks

4 cups cranberry juice

2 cups pineapple juice

Steps

1. Put the water, honey, cloves, and cinnamon sticks in the pot on the stovetop.

2. Heat the ingredients on high, stirring occasionally with the spoon. Bring to a **boil**, then reduce the heat to low and **simmer** for 25 minutes.

3. Turn off the heat. With the slotted spoon, remove the cinnamon sticks and cloves from the mixture and throw them away.

4. Add the cranberry and pineapple juices to the warm mixture and stir.

5. Remove the mixture from the stovetop with the pot holders and pour it into the punch bowl. Use the ladle to spoon the punch into mugs. May be served warm or cold.

Cloves are nail-shaped dried flower buds. The name *clove* comes from the Latin word *clavus*, which means "nail."

8

Perfect Pumpkin Nog

10 Minutes Prep Time	Tools	**2** 12-ounce servings

Ingredients

4 pitted whole dates

1 frozen banana

1 ½ cups **low-fat** milk (or almond milk)

8 ounces canned pumpkin (not pie filling)

2 teaspoons pure vanilla extract

½ teaspoon nutmeg

½ teaspoon cinnamon

Steps

1. Ask an adult to use the knife to cut the dates into small pieces on the cutting board.

2. Put the dates, frozen banana, and ½ cup of the milk in the blender. **Blend** on high for 30 seconds.

3. Add the pumpkin, the rest of the milk (1 cup), the vanilla extract, and the nutmeg and cinnamon. Blend 30 more seconds or until smooth.

4. Pour into 2 glasses.

Dates grow in thick **clusters** on the date palm tree, which is one of the world's oldest trees. This type of tree has been growing since at least the fifth century BC.

Health Tip

Dates are a good source of **vitamins** and **iron**.

9

Peppermint Hot Chocolate

5 Minutes Prep Time

Tools

2 Servings

Ingredients

1 peppermint candy cane

2 cups **low-fat** milk (or unsweetened soy milk)

2 tablespoons honey or agave

1 tablespoon pure vanilla extract

3 tablespoons unsweetened cocoa powder (more or less according to taste)

Optional: 2 marshmallows or 2 whole candy canes

Steps

1. Put the candy cane in a plastic bag and use the rolling pin to crush it.

2. In the pot, combine the milk, honey, and vanilla extract. Heat the ingredients over a medium flame on the stovetop.

3. Add the cocoa powder and stir with the spoon until it **dissolves**. Heat the mixture until it is hot, being careful not to **boil** it.

4. Add the crushed candy cane.

5. Using the pot holders, remove the pot from the stovetop and pour the mixture into the two mugs.

6. Optional: Top each mug with a marshmallow or put a candy cane in it.

fair trade Cocoa Powder

Cocoa beans are the fruit of the cacao tree. The beans were used as money in Latin America until the nineteenth century.

Health Tip

Cocoa has significant health benefits. Drinking cocoa decreases blood pressure, improves blood vessel health, and improves **cholesterol** levels.

Here We Come A-Wassailing Punch

25 Minutes Prep Time

15 Minutes Cooking Time

Tools

16 Servings

Ingredients

1 orange   1 lemon   1 gallon orange juice   10 cloves   6 cinnamon sticks

Steps

1 Ask an adult to use the knife to cut the orange and lemon into thin slices on the cutting board.

2 Put all the ingredients in a pot and stir them with the spoon. On the stovetop, bring the mixture to a **boil**. Then **simmer** over low heat until well heated, about 15 minutes.

3 Place the colander over the punch bowl. Using the pot holders, pour the mixture from the pot into the colander. The punch will be strained as it goes into the punch bowl.

4 Throw away the cinnamon sticks and the cloves. Put the orange and lemon slices in the punch bowl.

5 Use the ladle to spoon the punch into mugs. Drink it warm.

6 Refrigerate the leftover punch. When you feel like a warm drink, put the punch in a microwave-safe mug and heat for about 40 seconds or until warm.

Health Tip

The **nutrients** in oranges are many and varied. An orange is low in **calories**, contains no **cholesterol**, and is rich in dietary **fiber**.

The navel orange got its name from the "belly button" opposite the stem end. The bigger the navel, the sweeter the orange will be.

Valentine Pink Hot Cocoa

10 Minutes Prep Time

Tools

2 Servings

Ingredients

1 red beet

2 large marshmallows

2 tablespoons honey

2 cups **low-fat** milk

2 teaspoons unsweetened cocoa powder

Steps

1. Ask an adult to peel the beet using the peeler. Then use the knife to **slice** it in half on the cutting board.

2. Add the milk and beet to the pot and stir with the spoon. Bring the mixture to a **simmer** over a medium flame on the stovetop. Do not let it **boil**.

3. When the mixture is hot, turn off the heat. Use the slotted spoon to scoop out the beet and put it in a small bowl. Put the two marshmallows in the same bowl. With the spoon, rub the marshmallows over the beet to make them pink.

4. Using the pot holders, remove the pot from the flame and add the cocoa and honey to the milk mixture. Use a whisk to **blend** the ingredients together thoroughly.

5. Pour the mixture into the mugs. Top with the pink marshmallows. Throw away the beets.

Note: Adding more than 2 teaspoons of cocoa, for taste, will make the drink more brown than pink.

Both the root and the top leaves of the beet plant can be eaten.

St. Patrick's Day Green Smoothie

5 Minutes Prep Time

Tools  ②

2 Servings

Ingredients

1 cup orange juice

2 cups spinach

1 ripe banana

1 cup frozen pineapple

Steps

1. Pour the juice into the blender. Add the spinach and **blend** the ingredients until smooth, about 30 seconds.

2. Add the banana and the pineapple and blend until smooth, about 1 minute.

3. Pour the mixture into a tall glass. For a thicker shake, add another banana. For a less thick one, add more juice.

The American name for spinach comes from the Persian word *ispanai*, which means "green hand." It was later renamed *spanachia*, and eventually *spinach*.

Health Tip

Spinach is one of the world's healthiest vegetables. Rich in **vitamins** and **minerals**, it also gives you powerful **antioxidant** protection.

Sleepy Time Milk Tea

10 Minutes Prep Time

Tools

2 Servings

Ingredients

2 cups **low-fat** milk

½ teaspoon cinnamon

½ teaspoon nutmeg

1 teaspoon honey

Caffeine-free chamomile tea bag

caffeine free

Steps

1. Put the milk, cinnamon, nutmeg, and honey in a pot and stir with the spoon.

2. Cook the mixture over medium heat on the stovetop, being careful not to **boil** it.

3. When the mixture is warm, put a tea bag in the pot. Let the mixture **simmer** another 5 minutes.

4. Remove the tea bag with the spoon and discard.

5. Using the pot holders, pour the heated mixture into two mugs.

In *Peter Rabbit,* the famous children's book by Beatrix Potter, Peter can be found drinking chamomile tea when he is sick in bed at the end of the story.

HONEY

Wildflower

Apple Nut Oatmeal

10
Minutes
Prep Time

Tools

2
Servings

Health Tip

Oatmeal is healthy for your heart. To vary your oatmeal, use different nuts and fruit. Banana, apricots, agave, and pecans are all nutritious and delicious in oatmeal. Use your favorites.

Ingredients

½ Granny Smith apple

2 cups water

1 cup old-fashioned oats

½ teaspoon cinnamon

1 teaspoon honey

3 tablespoons walnut pieces

2 tablespoons raisins

Optional: milk

Steps

1. Peel the apple. Ask an adult to use the knife to cut out the **core** of the apple and discard it. Then have him or her cut the apple into small pieces on the cutting board.

2. Put the water and the oats in a pot.

3. Add the apple pieces and the cinnamon. Heat the ingredients over medium heat on the stovetop, stirring occasionally with the spoon.

4. When the mixture is cooked to the desired consistency (about 5 minutes), add the honey, walnut pieces, and raisins. Stir all the ingredients together.

5. Using the pot holders to hold the mixture, spoon the oatmeal into two small bowls. Add milk if desired.

In the early 1980s, the Quaker Oats Company declared January as the official oatmeal month. More oatmeal is bought in January than in any other month of the year.

Quick Corn Chowder

15 Minutes Prep Time

Tools

4 Servings

Ingredients

1 red bell pepper

1 small onion

2 ½ cups whole milk or almond milk

2 ½ cups frozen corn kernels

½ teaspoon salt

¼ teaspoon pepper

Steps

1. Ask an adult to use the knife to cut the red pepper in half on the cutting board. Remove the seeds and top and throw them away. **Dice** one half of the pepper. Refrigerate the other half for later use.

2. Peel the outer layer from the onion. Then **slice** the onion and cut the slices into small pieces.

3. Put the milk, onion pieces, and corn in the blender. **Blend** on high until smooth, about 1 minute.

4. Pour the corn mixture into the pot. Add the diced pepper and salt and pepper. Heat the ingredients in the pot on the stovetop until warm, about 5 minutes. Stir frequently with the large spoon. Do not **boil**.

5. Using the pot holders, pour the mixture into four soup bowls. May be served warm or cold.

Ethanol, a renewable **biofuel** made from corn, is currently blended into more than 80 percent of the nation's gasoline supply.

Butternut Squash Soup

25 Minutes Prep Time

1 Hour Cooking Time

Tools

6 Servings

Ingredients

2 medium butternut squashes (about 3 pounds)

1 ½ cups yellow onion pieces

2 Granny Smith apples

4 cups low-salt chicken stock

1 teaspoon sea salt

½ teaspoon black pepper

½ teaspoon nutmeg

1 cup apple juice

Optional: shredded apple for decoration

Health Tip

Use this hearty winter squash as a healthy **carbohydrate** choice in place of rice or pasta. Try different spices such as cumin, rosemary, or thyme in place of the nutmeg.

Steps

1. Ask an adult to peel the squash and scrape out the seeds. Discard the seeds. Then use the knife to cut the **flesh** into 2-inch cubes on the cutting board.

2. **Dice** the onions.

3. Peel, core, and cut the apples into small pieces.

4. Put the squash, apples, and onion pieces in the pot on the stovetop.

5. Pour the chicken stock into the pot. Add the salt, pepper, and nutmeg, and stir.

6. Bring to a **boil**, then reduce the heat and **simmer** for 45 minutes.

7. Turn off the heat. Remove the pot from the stovetop with pot holders. Sit it on a heat-resistant surface. Allow the mixture to cool slightly.

8. Pour small batches of the soup into the blender and **blend** until smooth. After blending each batch, put it in the large bowl.

9. Pour the blended soup from the bowl back into the pot. Add the apple juice and heat the mixture until hot.

10. Use the ladle to spoon the mixture into soup bowls. Decorate with shredded apple if desired.

Many years ago, people only ate the seeds of the squash, not the flesh. You can lightly salt the seeds and roast them like pumpkin seeds.

Ginger Cookies

20 Minutes Prep Time

10–12 Minutes Cooking Time

Tools

30–36 Servings

Health Tip

Ginger is widely used in the treatment of medical problems. It is used to treat everything from the common cold to migraines.

Ingredients

Cooking spray

¾ cup unsalted butter (or coconut oil)

¾ cup sugar

1 egg

¼ cup dark molasses

1 cup sifted all-purpose flour

1 cup sifted whole wheat flour

2 teaspoons baking soda

1 tablespoon ground ginger

1 teaspoon ground cinnamon

½ teaspoon salt

Steps

1. **Preheat** the oven to 350°F. Lightly coat the cookie sheet with the cooking spray.

2. Put the butter and sugar in the large bowl. Use the electric mixer to **blend** the ingredients until smooth. Crack the egg on the side of the bowl, let it slide in, and mix until light and fluffy.

3. Pour in the molasses.

4. Put the flours, baking soda, ginger, cinnamon, and salt in a medium bowl. Use the spoon to mix them together.

5. Add the flour mixture to the liquid ingredients and use the mixer to blend until well combined.

6. With a tablespoon, scoop dough into small 1-inch balls. Place each ball on the greased cookie sheet 2 inches apart.

7. Bake 10 to 12 minutes, until the cookies have spread out and the tops have cracked.

8. Carefully remove the cookie sheet from the oven with the pot holders. With the spatula, move the cookies to the wire rack to cool.

whole wheat Flour

ginger

Ginger is an effective treatment for nausea associated with motion sickness.

Yummy Coconut Balls

15 Minutes Prep Time

Tools

20 1-inch balls

Ingredients

½ cup walnuts

½ cup almonds

½ cup pitted dates

2 tablespoons cocoa powder

½ cup maple syrup

½ cup creamy peanut butter

½ teaspoon pure vanilla extract

¼ teaspoon sea salt

1 cup shredded unsweetened coconut (may use regular coconut)

Steps

1. Have an adult set up the food processor with the S blade. Put the walnuts and almonds in the food processor. Mix until coarsely ground, about 30 seconds.

2. Add the dates and mix until the nuts and dates are well combined, about 20 seconds.

3. Add the cocoa powder, maple syrup, peanut butter, vanilla extract, and salt. Mix until the ingredients are smooth and thick.

4. Use the spoon to help pour the mixture into a medium bowl. With your hands, roll pieces of the mixture into 1-inch balls. Place the balls on wax paper.

5. Put the shredded coconut on a small plate. Roll each ball in the coconut until fully coated. Put all the balls in a sealed container in the freezer. Eat them right out of the freezer.

A coconut is one of the largest known seeds in the world. When a coconut falls from a palm tree, it takes about three years for the seed to take root and sprout into a new tree.

Nut-and-Honey Bars

15 Minutes Prep Time

20–25 Minutes Cooking Time

Tools

21 Bars

Health Tip

You can use coconut oil as a healthy substitute for butter in this recipe, and in place of the cooking spray to grease the pan.

Ingredients

Cooking spray
½ cup cashews
1 ½ cups pumpkin seeds

1 cup almonds
½ cup sunflower seeds
1 cup dried cranraisins

1 teaspoon cinnamon
½ cup honey
¼ cup butter (½ stick)

Steps

1. **Preheat** the oven to 350°F. Coat a 9 X 13-inch casserole dish with cooking spray.

2. Have an adult set up the food processor with the S blade. Put the cashews, 1 cup of the pumpkin seeds, and the almonds into the food processor. **Grind** into flour (about 40 seconds). Don't grind too long or the mixture will turn into butter.

3. With the mixing spoon, put the nut flour into a medium bowl. Add the sunflower seeds, ½ cup of pumpkin seeds, cranraisins, and cinnamon into the bowl and stir.

4. On the stovetop, put the butter and honey in a pot and heat until the butter melts.

5. Carefully remove the pot from the stovetop with the potholders and pour the honey mixture over the nut mixture. Stir until everything is evenly coated.

6. Pour the mixture into the casserole dish. Use a wet spoon to spread it evenly.

7. Bake for 20 to 25 minutes, until it is lightly browned on top.

8. Carefully remove the dish from the oven with the pot holders. Let the mixture cool for 20 minutes, then gently cut it into bars. Allow the bars to cool completely before removing them from the pan with a spatula.

Cashews are in the same family as poison ivy and poison sumac. They have chemical irritants, but those are only found in the shell and not in the nut itself. To make sure that the cashews are free of these irritants, manufacturers **roast** the nuts at a very high temperature.

Nutty Crunchy Granola

Tools

Ingredients

2 cups old-fashioned oats

½ cup **slivered** almonds

½ cup chopped pecans

½ cup raw sunflower seeds

3 tablespoons creamy peanut butter

¼ cup honey

½ teaspoon pure vanilla extract

½ tablespoon ground cinnamon

½ cup unsweetened shredded coconut (may also use sweetened coconut)

½ cup raisins or any other dried fruit

Health Tip

Whole grain oats make this granola a heart healthy food.

Steps

1. **Preheat** the oven to 300°F.

2. In the large bowl, stir together the oats, almonds, pecans, and seeds with the mixing spoon.

3. In the small bowl, mix together the peanut butter and honey. Microwave the mixture for 30 seconds, then stir it with the spoon. Add the vanilla extract and cinnamon to the peanut butter mixture and stir until the ingredients are combined.

4. Pour the liquid mixture into the nut mixture and mix well with the spoon.

5. Spread the mixture onto the ungreased cookie sheet and bake for 10 minutes.

6. Carefully remove the cookie sheet from the oven with the pot holders. Clean the spoon. Then stir the mixture and sprinkle the shredded coconut on top. Return the cookie sheet to the oven and heat for 10 more minutes.

7. Remove the cookie sheet from the oven. Stir in raisins or any other dried fruit.

8. Cool the mixture completely. Use the spatula to remove the mixture from the cookie sheet. Place it in a plastic bag or other container. The mixture will keep for a month.

9. Sprinkle Nutty Crunchy Granola on cereal, yogurt, ice cream, fruit, or eat it on its own.

Granola is often eaten by hikers because it is lightweight, a good source of energy, and easy to store.

Healthy Tips

Nutrition Facts
Serving Size 5 oz. (144g)
Servings Per Container 4

Amount Per Serving

Calories 310   Calories from Fat 100

% Daily Value*

Total Fat 15g   21%
Saturated Fat 2.6g   13%
Trans Fat 1g
Cholesterol 118mg   39%
Sodium 560mg   28%
Total Carbohydrate 12g   4%
Dietary Fiber 1g   4%
Sugars 1g
Protein 24g

Vitamin A 2%   •   Vitamin C 2%
Calcium 2%   •   Iron 5%

* Percent Daily Values are based on a 2,000 calorie
diet. Your daily values may be higher or lower
depending on your calorie needs:

	Calories	2,000	2,500
Total Fat	Less Than	65g	80g
Saturated Fat	Less Than	20g	25g
Cholesterol	Less Than	300mg	300mg
Sodium	Less Than	2,400mg	2,400mg
Total Carbohydrate		300g	375g
Dietary Fiber		25g	30g

Calories per gram:
Fat 9   •   Carbohydrate 4   •   Protein 4

Always Read Labels

Labels on packaging tell how much fat, sugar, **vitamins**, and other **nutrients** are in food. If you compare one bottle of juice with another, for example, you can determine which one has fewer **calories**, less sugar, and so on. Don't forget to look at the serving size when comparing foods.

Make Recipe Substitutions

While all the recipes in this book call for wholesome ingredients, you can make even healthier snacks by substituting some ingredients for others. For example:

- Dairy: use nonfat or **low-fat** instead of full fat when it comes to dairy products such as yogurt, cheese, sour cream, and milk. Use soy or almond milk instead of cow's milk. Coconut oil may be used in place of butter.

- Salt: choose "lightly salted" or "no salt added" nuts to reduce **sodium** content. Reduce the salt in recipes according to taste.

- Juice: choose 100 percent fruit juice or juice with no added sugar.

- Sugar: use honey, agave, or maple syrup instead of sugar in recipes.

- Fruit: if fresh fruit is unavailable, use frozen unsweetened fruit.

Glossary

antioxidant (an-tee-OK-suh-duhnt) one of several substances in certain foods that may prevent cell damage, which can cause disease in people and animals

biofuel (BY-oh-*fyoo*-uhl) a type of fuel made from living animal or plant matter

blend (BLEND) to mix two or more ingredients together

boil (BOIL) to heat up a liquid until it starts to bubble

calories (KAL-uh-reez) measurements of the amount of energy that food provides

carbohydrate (car-bo-HIGH-drate) a source of energy for the body that includes foods containing starches and sugars

cholesterol (kuh-LESS-tuh-*rol*) a fatty substance people need to digest food; too much in the blood can increase the chance of heart disease

clusters (KLUH-stirs) groups of similar things growing close together in bunches

core (KOR) the hard center of an apple or pear where the seeds are found

dice (DICE) to cut into small cubes

dissolves (di-SOLVES) to break apart a solid and make it disappear into a liquid

fiber (FYE-bur) a substance found in parts of plants that when eaten passes through the body but is not completely digested; it helps food move through one's intestines and is important for good health

flesh (FLESH) the part of a fruit or vegetable that is eaten

grind (GRIND) to reduce to small particles by crushing

immunity (ih-MYOON-ity) bodily power to resist an ailment or disease

iron (EYE-urn) a mineral found in foods such as meat, eggs, and dried fruit; it helps move oxygen from the lungs to the rest of the body

low-fat (*loh*-FAT) food that has three or fewer grams of fat per serving

minerals (MIN-ur-uhlz) chemical substances, such as iron or zinc, that occur naturally in certain foods and are important for good health

nutrients (NOO-tree-uhnts) things that are found in food and are needed by people and animals to stay healthy

obesity (oh-BEESS-ih-tee) a condition where a person is extremely overweight

preheat (pree-HEET) to turn on an oven and allow it to heat up to a specific temperature before using

pre-made (PREE-mayd) already prepared

preservatives (pri-ZUR-vuh-tivz) chemicals put into foods to keep them from spoiling

roast (ROHST) to cook in a hot oven

simmer (SIM-ur) to boil slowly at a low temperature

slice (SLYES) to cut into thin, flat pieces

slivered (SLIHVERD) cut into small, narrow pieces

sodium (SOH-dee-uhm) a chemical found in salt that the body needs in small amounts; too much salt in one's diet can cause health problems

vitamins (VYE-tuh-minz) substances in food that are necessary for good health

Index

almonds 19, 21
apple 15, 17
apple juice 17
baking soda 18
banana 9, 13, 15
beet 12
bell pepper 16
butter 18, 20, 22
candy canes 10

cashews 20
chamomile tea 14
chicken stock 17
cinnamon 9, 14, 15, 18, 20, 21
cinnamon sticks 8, 11
cloves 8, 11
cocoa 10, 12, 19

coconut 19, 21
corn 16
cranberry 8
cranraisins 20
dates 9, 19
flour 18
ginger 18
honey 8, 10, 12, 14, 15, 20, 21, 22

lemon 11
maple syrup 19, 22
marshmallows 10, 12
milk 9, 10, 12, 14, 15, 16, 22
nutmeg 9, 14, 17
oats 15, 21

onion 16, 17
orange 11
orange juice 11, 13
peanut butter 19, 21
pecans 21
pineapple 13
pineapple juice 8
pumpkin 9

pumpkin seeds 17, 20
raisins 15, 21
spinach 13
sugar 18, 22
sunflower seeds 20, 21
vanilla extract 9, 10, 19, 21
walnuts 15, 19

Bibliography

Chef AJ and Glen Merzer. *Unprocessed: How to Achieve Vibrant Health and Your Ideal Weight.* Charleston, SC: Kale Publishing (2011).

Yolen, Jane and Heidi E. Y. Stemple. *Fairy Tale Desserts: A Cookbook for Young Readers and Eaters.* New York, NY: Windmill Books (2009).

Read More

Butterworth, Chris. *How Did That Get In MY Lunchbox?: The Story of Food.* Somerville, MA: Candlewick (2011).

Raabe, Emily. *A Christmas Holiday Cookbook.* New York, NY: Rosen Publishing Group (2002).

Raabe, Emily. *A Passover Holiday Cookbook.* New York, NY: Rosen Publishing Group (2003).

Learn More Online

To learn more about making winter treats
www.bearportpublishing.com/YummyTummyRecipes-Seasons

About the Author

Marilyn LaPenta has been a teacher for more than 25 years and has published numerous works for teachers and students. She has always enjoyed cooking with her students and her three children, and looks forward to cooking with her three grandchildren. Marilyn lives in Brightwaters, New York.